Good News /
Bad News

Good News/ Bad News

HENRY MARTIN

CHARLES SCRIBNER'S SONS · NEW YORK

Library of Congress Cataloging in Publication Data
Martin, Henry R
    Good news/bad news.
    1. Business—Caricatures and cartoons.   2.   American
wit and humor, Pictorial.   I.   Title.

NC1429.M4242A46   741.5'973   76–41348
ISBN 0–684–14844–7

1 3 5 7 9 11 13 15 17 19 V/C 20 18 16 14 12 10 8 6 4 2

PRINTED IN THE UNITED STATES OF AMERICA

To Edie. Ann and Jane with love

Foreword

It was nineteen thirty-two.

'Pretty Face' Martin and 'Fat Annie' Hagan had been mowed down in front of Grundy County Savings and Loan, Hope, Kentucky. A vacuum formed in the gas tank of their Model A Ford at get-away time.

The Martin family, a closely-knit group for many generations decided that little six-year-old nephew Henry was to receive 'Pretty Face's' shoes, dog Wolf and some pencils. The shoes, of course, were too large for little Henry but they were an expensive pair of brown and white Adler elevateds well worth the keeping. Little Henry became fond of the shoes, Wolf and the pencils. A few short weeks later Wolf ran amuck and was hit by a train. Henry drew closer to the shoes and began sketching pictures with his pencils. Time passed. Henry was destined to attend Princeton University. He continued sketching all through his school years and was graduated Phi Cum Laud Adler Elevateds.

In time The New Yorker magazine was to take notice of Henry's pictures and publish Henry Martin in two hundred and twenty-four countries around the World.

'Pretty Face' would have been proud.

George Booth. © 1976

A cat for Sir Henry!

BOOTH

Good News/
Bad News

"Get up, Harry, or you'll be late for work and a liberated woman will get your job."

"This is the first day of the rest of your life, old chap! I think that calls for a little celebration. How about a double Martini with lunch?"

"Congratulations on quitting smoking. Congratulations on passing up Martinis at lunch. Congratulations on avoiding heavy desserts. And last, but not least, congratulations on those fancy new sideburns."

"Hi, there, the me nobody knows!"

"The egg timer is pinging. The toaster is popping. The coffeepot is perking. Is this it, Alice? Is this the great American dream?"

"Harry, is there anything we, as a couple, should be doing
about National Pickle Week?"

"A little travelling music, if you please, Margaret."

"Well, dear, have a nice day at your office, club, and tryst."

"Good morning, cubicle!"

"Good morning, vice-presidents!"

"Xerox Corporation. How do you
do and how do you do and how do
you do again?"

"I am Account No. 327-94-33AT, and I would like
a word with your computer."

"Here at Compudata, Inc., Mr. Waycross, our
motto is: Analyze, systemize, computerize,
synthesize, finalize, and make a bundle."

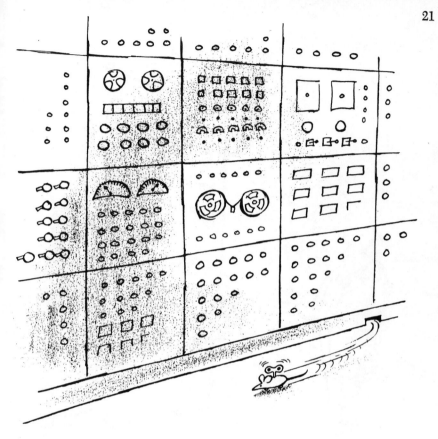

H. Martin

"No matter what ecological data we feed in, the print-out always reads: 'It's too late to save me, just save yourself.'"

"One of us has got to go, Jenson. There isn't room in
this company for two electronic wizards."

"Bradley, are you visualizing, synthesizing, conceptualizing, analyzing, finalizing, or catching up on your sleep?"

"And when you're finished with those, Miss Nedley,
you can Xerox yourself for me."

"I'm sorry, sir, but B. J. Mogmire, Inc., no longer accepts over-the-transom business."

"While you're waiting, would you like to read a sampling
of our inter-office memos?"

"Memo to all salesmen: damn the recession—full speed ahead!"

"Mr. Gregory, come quick! The Accounting Department
is switched on and love is everywhere!"

"As we feared, Harkness was stunned by the news."

"Mr. Sloane, the directors are seated in the conference room waiting for you to make your grand entrance with humble apologies for keeping them waiting."

"Each of you has been provided with a pad of paper and a pencil should you care to take notes, jot down ideas, make memorandums, doodle, play tic-tac-toe, or pass each other funny notes."

"Gentlemen, I have some extremely good news to report!"

"But before we throw the meeting open for discussion, Ed Fenton
wants to show you the buck and wing he learned at last week's
EDC Convention in Atlantic City."

"Gentlemen, I have good news and bad news."

"Damn it, will whoever keeps saying 'Pshaw'
please refrain until the treasurer has finished his report?"

"Gentlemen, I'm happy to announce that the all-expense-paid two-weeks' tour of Europe has been awarded to Ms. Feona Putts in the Chicago office for her winning suggestion that a 10 percent raise be approved for the board of directors."

"Now, depending on <u>how</u> we read these accounting figures,
we have either an excess profit or an excess deficit."

"To illustrate my point, gentlemen, I'm going to tell a little joke, and I want you to laugh at it as if you'd never heard it before and your job depended upon it."

"First of all, I'd like to welcome two new members to the board."

"Will whoever's smoking pot kindly refrain until
the major issues have been voted on?"

"If Trend-Dec, Inc., will propose a two-for-one split,
knock three times."

"Name?"   "Robert Warren McLaughlin III."
"Address?"   "East Sixties."
"Religion?"   "Episcopalian."
"Schools?"   "Exeter, Yale."
"Clothes?"   "Brooks Brothers."
"Golf?"   "Low seventies."
"Hired!"

"How would you like to start at the top? We have an opening for a chairman of the board of a beleaguered and bankrupt railroad."

"Excuse me, but is this the office for separating the sheep from the goats or is this the office for separating the men from the boys?"

"A word to the wise, Bodner. In this morning's meeting, you were referred to as 'a certain party who shall remain nameless.'"

"En garde, Larkins. An equally qualified cutie pie
is after your job."

"For what it's worth, Malloy, you've been reclassified as dead wood."

"Right now I'm afraid a promotion is out of the question, Walters, but I can say that we no longer consider you personnel but part of the Dymanell family."

"I'm sorry, Maypother, but I've pushed the 'down' button for you."

"It is with a deep sense of personal regret that, after a close relationship of ten warm, wonderful years, I must tender my resignation, Dum-Dum!"

"The trick is to have enough to ask the old man for a raise
but not enough to get yourself fired and blow it."

"I'm firing you, Comstock, because I don't like the cut of your jib."

"Carpenter is being transferred to a new division."

"That's Ted Mason. He's waiting for his big opportunity."

"I'm sorry but Mr. Bradley can't be disturbed right now.
He's busy shaping company policy, setting up guidelines,
evaluating field reports, and stuff like that."

"Damn it, Carlson, I told you if you put <u>Ms.</u> Thompson and <u>Mrs.</u> Keller in the same cubicle together there would be wall-to-wall trouble!"

"International Servico Incorporated's the name.
Conglomerchandising's the game."

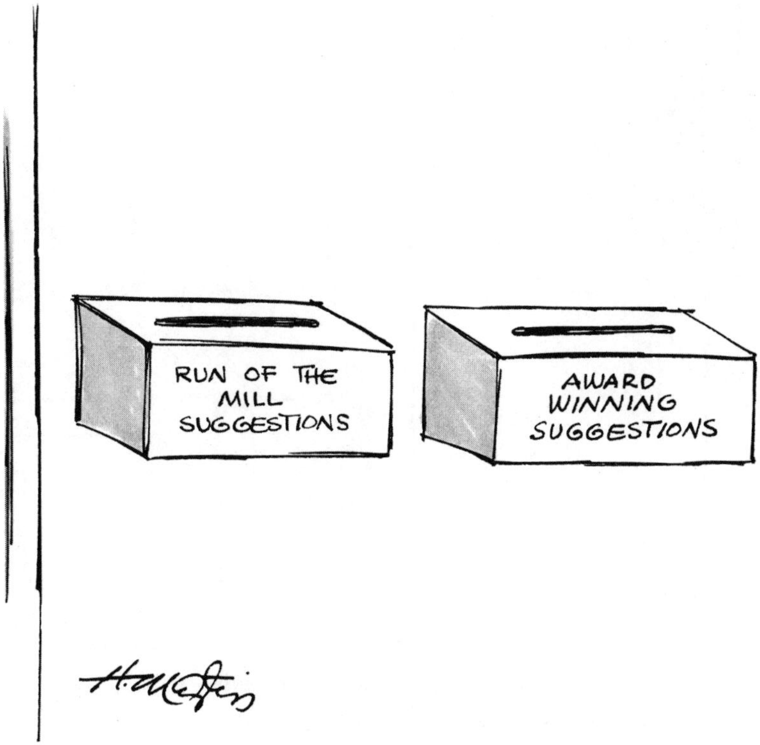
RUN OF THE
MILL
SUGGESTIONS
AWARD
WINNING
SUGGESTIONS

"I'm going to close the door for a few minutes, Miss Beckerman,
while I make a few mysterious phone calls."

"When you've worked with him as long as I have you gradually become aware that underneath that gruff exterior there beats a heart of cold steel."

"Besides your scheduled appointments there are a disgruntled employee, an enraged stockholder, an enlightened consumer advocate, an irate customer, and a persistent insurance salesman waiting to see you."

"Edsie! What are you doing out of uniform?"

"J.B., I want your job in the worst way."

"On behalf of the Audubon Society I want to thank you for your recent corporate contribution and the responsible attitude you and others in your industry are taking toward matters ecological."

"Buy Texas Gulf Sulphur!"

"Never mind all that price-earnings ratio stuff. Just put me down for 100 shares of IBM to win, 100 shares of Xerox to place, and 100 shares of AT&T to show."

"I wish for all the dazzling trappings of success
with none of the responsibilities."

71

"I wish for that rare quality so often found in
truly great men—ambition without greed."

"I wish I were rich, handsome, well tailored and well groomed, gracious, elegant, dashing, distinguished, and yet much admired by my peers."

"My principal thrust this year has been to continue to build my expertise and to understand and service customer needs even better. I've tried to solicit new business aggressively and place an even higher priority on expanding and intensifying relationships with my broad base of existing customers in a period of high inflation."

"What can you recommend that's low in fat, high
in protein, and fit for a king?"

"Tod Blaker's firm is headquartered in New York, but I believe
he and Sally are domiciled in White Plains."

"Ted, Jr., works for the Chemical Bank, which you may remember was the Chemical Bank New York Trust Company before changing its name from the Chemical Corn Exchange Bank after becoming Chemical Bank and Trust Company, previously called the Chemical National Bank of New York, which was first called the Chemical Bank."

"Well, from his letters we know that in the two short years Ralph, Jr., has been in San Francisco, he's gained a wide reputation in certain quarters making the biggies really sit up and take notice and that offers are pouring in from all over permitting him a free choice in all future commitments. Beyond that, we haven't a clue as to what the child is doing."

"I'll have the 'Businessman's Lunch' and she'll have the 'Just
a Housewife's Lunch.'"

"Hey, it was good to see you, Spence, and remember me to your wife and families."

"This one's for keeping a neat and tidy cubicle at all times and this one's for not tying up lines with personal calls and this one's for not horsing around at the water cooler."

"I don't want a raise, Mr. Harlingen. I just want bouquets and accolades and tokens of esteem and bravos and huzzahs and a piece of the action."

"Hello! What's this?"

"I'm grateful for your offer, but how would it sound to the tax examiner when I said, 'A little fairy brought me the swimming pool, the Bentley, and the cabin cruiser'?"

"Well, don't just sit there. Xerox something."

"Dear Lord! Why don't <u>my</u> ball-point
pens ever work?"

"Good morning, Miss Shefferman. I just wanted you to know I've finished my yoga, yogurt, and meditation and am ready for commerce, communication, and come what may."

"Miss Tompkins, connect me with somebody."

"Miss Spellman, send in a vice-president who can work well under a man who, though admittedly is difficult to get along with, is undeniably a genius."

"Good morning, Mr. Carrington. The story thus far: Miss Redfield, your secretary, is on vacation. Filling in for Miss Redfield is Mrs. Booker, who fell ill yesterday. Substituting for Mrs. Booker is Ms. Stollman, who is on her lunch break. Pinch-hitting for Ms. Stollman is Miss Luray, who is in the ladies' room. I'm Mrs. Colwin covering for Miss Luray. May I help you?"

"Miss Garman, bring in the actuary tables, the Old Farmer's Almanac, the day-by-day horoscope, the Ouija board, the cards, and the crystal ball."

"Miss Granger, I'd like to see the following in my office immediately: my lawyers, my financial wizard, my tax men, my right-hand man, two yes men, three vice-presidents, my fair-haired boy, my whipping boy, and old what's-his-name in accounting."

"Miss Barringer, send in somebody to mark my words."

"Miss Taylor, were there any garbled messages while I was out?"

"Is your lens capable of capturing the simple quality and inner strength so often found in men who achieve success at an early age and who manage to hang on to it throughout a busy and productive lifetime?"

"You are a pompous, conceited, bombastic, pretentious old windbag."

"This is my executive suite and this is my executive vice-president, Ralph Anderson, and my executive secretary, Adele Eades, and my executive desk and my executive carpet and my executive wastebasket and my executive ashtray and my executive pen set and my . . ."

"Oh, come in, J.B. I'd like you to meet my executive suite-mate, Terry Anderson."

". . . and this is Jeff Hinson, my left-hand man."

"Believe me, gang. Just because I've been given my own cubicle doesn't mean I'm going to forget my old friends."

HAPPINESS IS A
PIECE OF
THE ACTION

"Confound it, Miss Avery! Where is my stamp of approval?"

"Mr. Stewart is out of his gourd at the moment.
May I take a message?"

"Look, could you come to our next research-and-development meeting and tell them just what you've told me?"

"No cause for worry, Miss Aiken. I'll burn that bridge
when I come to it."

"Good heavens, Mr. Perkins, are you on something?"

"I just wanted to know if there was any chance First National might be willing to forgive my debts as I forgive my debtors."

"Let me just make a little note of that. I never seem to get anything done around here unless I make little notes."

"To be perfectly frank, I've been trying so long to get hold of you that I've forgotten who you are and what I'm calling about."

"This is Arthur Rumson. Sorry you reached me so abruptly, but my secretary is out sick, my answering service is on strike, and my Phone-Mate is in the shop."

"The time is 2:15 P.M. The temperature is 70. The air is acceptable. The weather is perfect. The sun is shining. The market is up. The times are good. The living is easy. The vibes are zingy and the ambience is 97 percent and rising."

"Hi there, vendee. This is vendor."

124

"Oh, nothing much. I just called to say hello and see how you're getting along and to find out how Alice and the kids are and to see how your new house is progressing and to sell you a homeowner's policy."

"It's been nice talking to you, and remember me to your present wife."

"Miss Wendell, has any news reached our office today
that calls for a little drink?"

"Emily, I've just cleared my desk and am taking the afternoon off."

"Miss Stouffer, I'm closing up shop for the day. Will you check me out? Shredder off. Automatic conversation-monitor off. Phone-Mate off. Executive-dictation unit off. Electric stapler off. . . ."

"Louie, I've just been promoted to vice-president and treasurer, so from now on instead of 'What'll it be, Mac?' could you say, 'The usual, Mr. Dougherty?'"

"Ode to a dedicated executive who labors far into a moonless night long after his staff have deserted their posts to while away their frivolous lives in idle play."

"I thought you'd be interested to know that I'm just about to go off the deep end!"

"Now here's one that'll really cheer him up."

"These days, I suppose, air-conditioning breakdown must be regarded as one of the facts of life."

"Dear Classmate: Old Annual Giving time is here again, so whip out your checkbook and rush off a fat one to us. The sooner you do this the faster we'll get off your neck with repeated mailings and frequent phone calls and that's a promise.

Sincerely yours,

Binkey Toddwyler, '48 Fund Chairman"

"Spooky!"   "Flat top!"

". . . but by the time you discover the loss of your credit card it will be too late. Someone will have had a swinging $8,275.24 two weeks in gay, carefree, sun-drenched Acapulco."

"Well, this year, Mother, we're trying separate vacations. I'm going to Barbados with the girls while Ralph, as Telix Incorporated's newly appointed chairman of the board, is off on an ego trip."

"Philsie, this is M. J. I hate like hell to bother you while you're on vacation, but something has come up."

OUR VACATION WAS MADE POSSIBLE THROUGH A GRANT FROM MOBIL OIL

"Now this will be our reception room, and this, the conference room, and over here will be daddy's executive suite."

"Get your *Wall Street Journal, Advertising Age, Women's Wear Daily,*
Variety, Sales Management . . ."

"That's as close as Harry
ever gets to relaxing."

"Farewell, fun seekers! I must return to my people!"

"Well, I guess that wraps up the Labor Day weekend."

"It's hard to believe it's October already."

"I'll have the Number 2 Dinner, the 'Thanksgiving Feast for Lonely Executives Trapped in the City on Business, Unable to Be at Home with Family and Friends,' with pumpkin pie and coffee later."

"Gimme, gimme, gimme!"

"Season's Greetings from the Mackhold Agency. Season's Greetings from Coleman Oil Company. Season's Greetings from Brian, Thurlo, McCreedy, Kaufman & Grouse. Season's Greetings from Wade International. Season's Greetings from G. R. Preston Incorporated. Season's Greetings from . . ."

"Good morning, Ms. Judson. It is time once again for you to remind Mr. Carlson that it is Christmas bonus time and being such let's not forget the night crew who labor while you sleep to keep your office clean, neat, and tidy."

"Miss Hexley, have some old and trusted employees
drop by to wish me a Merry Christmas."

"I know it's wrong of me, Sid, but I love the vulgarity
of commercial Christmasism."

"Now, while we're dancing, let's all be thinking how we can step up doll production, cut costs in the toy car division, and eliminate waste in all departments."

"O.K., men, time to halt regular production and switch to
stocking stuffers and last-minute suggestions."

"Ho! Ho! Ho! Jenkins—you're fired!"

"I'm afraid I don't know what it is either, dear, but the ad said it was the perfect gift for office or den."

"This is my workshop, Mother. These are my tools.
Here I tinker and putter in the world of finance."

"Listen, Sonny, if I don't remind you to schedule the annual stockholders meeting or take a fresh look at the location of key distribution centers or check into present handling of your overall accounting procedures then what's a mother for?"

"Dear Sonny:

Thank you for the copy of your annual report. Your father and I are mighty proud of the good job you're doing as president of such a big outfit. However, we thought you looked tired in the picture of you opposite the president's report. Have you been getting enough rest and exercise? Are you taking your vitamins, and is that daughter-in-law of ours fixing you good, nourishing meals?"

"Before we head into the annual meeting, gentlemen, I thought a quick little review of just who we are might be in order."

"Happy days are here again.
The shares you hold have split again.
We plan to raise the dividend.
Happy days are here again!"

"Wow! Let's see. First, I'd like to have more say in the day-to-day running of this organization. Second, I'd like to see my good buddy Larry Johnson given a free hand to run the Ward Bellco division. And third, I'd like to stop these daydreams and make better use of this time getting red-hot ideas that will bring me a raise and a promotion."

"Try as I may, Charles, I find it difficult to believe that
you are the same Charles A. Glackman who is chairman
of the board of Marcar International Incorporated."

"Alice, do you have great ambitions for me or is treasurer of R. T. Caulkins Company, Inc., as far as I'm going?"

"Congratulations, Mr. Dellington! You've made it to the top."

"If it's so lonely at the top, Mr. Blivins, why don't
you go back to the bottom?"

"In 1948, he was made vice-president and treasurer. Then, in 1953, he was promoted to president and director. In 1960, he was named chairman of the board, and then, last Friday, in an unprecedented move, he was apotheosized."

"Live and learn! I thought being 'kicked upstairs' was
always just a figure of speech."

"Here's a thought: Instead of kicking old J.B. upstairs,
why don't we just kick him out?"

"Miss Lawler, at the end of next month I am retiring. Please inform the board of directors and the company retirement fund of this decision. Also, send yourself a dozen red roses. Card to read: To Miss Lawler—Sincerest thanks for twenty years of devoted service. Affectionately, Frank W."

"Gentlemen, this is my last meeting. I am tendering my resignation and request 15 minutes at the close of this busy agenda for some maudlin reminiscences, exchange of wet-eyed glances, heartfelt handclasps, and mawkish farewells."

"Wait a second, Senior Citizen! You
retired yesterday. Remember?"

"During the current recession, Mildred has been my fortress."

"We've had our ups and downs, Jeremy, but
overall it's been a good marriage."

"Instead of sitting around watching TV, shouldn't you be studying your portfolio, weeding out the dogs and the weak sisters, and looking for some low-priced growth potentials?"

"Hocus-pocus dominocus. I turn you into a happy, warmhearted, agreeable person."

"That was our answering service, saying they join Martha and John's answering service, and Sonny and Marvin's answering service, in wishing us a happy anniversary."

"You're pushing sixty, Sanford. Is there anything you can look back on and say it was your finest hour?"

"Give it to me straight, Doc. Are all systems go?"

"My joints ache, my hair seems to be going,
I've been noticing crow's-feet around my eyes.
Doc, what's happening to me?"

"I must say that what Harry may lack in charisma he makes up for in IBM, Xerox, and Standard Oil of New Jersey."

"My Protestant work ethic made me a bundle, but my
Puritanical guilt complex won't let me enjoy it."

H. Martin

"This country may be on the wrong track, Leland,
but your wearing a long face twenty-four hours a day,
seven days a week, fifty-two weeks a year isn't going
to help set it on the right track."

"The dear thing. He's back at some bygone convention, or some half-forgotten sales conference long ago."

Sources

PAGE

1. *Saturday Review,*
   January 11, 1975
2. *The New Yorker,*
   February 17, 1975
3. *The New Yorker,* June 3, 1972
4. *The New Yorker,* April 11, 1970
5. *The New Yorker,*
   September 18, 1971
6. *The New Yorker,* January 6, 1973
7. *The New Yorker,* May 24, 1969
8. *The New Yorker,* July 21, 1975
9. *The New Yorker,*
   February 16, 1976
10. Previously unpublished
11. *The New Yorker,* June 15, 1968
12. *Saturday Review,* May 6, 1972
13. *The New Yorker,* July 13, 1968
14. Previously unpublished
15. Previously unpublished
16. *The New Yorker,*
    September 16, 1967
17. *The New Yorker,* April 13, 1968
18. *The New Yorker,* July 22, 1967
19. *The New Yorker,*
    November 21, 1970
20. *The New Yorker,* May 25, 1968
21. *Datamation,* September 15, 1971
22. *Saturday Review,*
    August 22, 1970
23. *The New Yorker,*
    January 16, 1971
24. *Saturday Review,* July 13, 1973
25. *The New Yorker,*
    November 28, 1970
26. *Saturday Review,*
    October 10, 1972
27. Previously unpublished
28. *Saturday Review,* May 17, 1975
29. *The New Yorker,* March 28, 1970
30. Previously unpublished
31. Previously unpublished
32. Previously unpublished
33. Previously unpublished
34. Previously unpublished
35. Previously unpublished
36. Previously unpublished
37. *The New Yorker,* May 27, 1967
38. Previously unpublished
39. *The New Yorker,*
    February 2, 1976
40. Previously unpublished
41. *Saturday Review,* March 8, 1975
42. *Sales Management,*
    December 15, 1969
43. *Saturday Review,*
    October 16, 1971
44. Previously unpublished
45. *Saturday Review,*
    February 9, 1974
46. Previously unpublished
47. *The New Yorker,*
    December 8, 1975
48. Previously unpublished
49. Previously unpublished
50. Previously unpublished
51. Previously unpublished
52. *Better Homes & Gardens,*
    July 1971
53. Previously unpublished
54. *Saturday Review,*
    January 25, 1975
55. Previously unpublished
56. Previously unpublished
57. Previously unpublished
58. Previously unpublished
59. Previously unpublished
60. Previously unpublished
61. Previously unpublished
62. Previously unpublished
63. Previously unpublished
64. Previously unpublished
65. Previously unpublished

66. Previously unpublished
67. Previously unpublished
68. *The New Yorker,*
    October 29, 1966
69. *Saturday Review,* July 13, 1974
70. *The New Yorker,*
    November 4, 1967
71. *The New Yorker,* August 9, 1969
72. *The New Yorker,* April 3, 1971
73. *The New Yorker,*
    November 18, 1967
74. *The New Yorker,* October 7, 1967
75. Previously unpublished
76. *Saturday Review,* April 19, 1975
77. Previously unpublished
78. *The New Yorker,* July 30, 1973
79. *The New Yorker,*
    September 8, 1975
80. Previously unpublished
81. Previously unpublished
82. Previously unpublished
83. *The New Yorker,*
    December 15, 1975
84. *The New Yorker,* January 7, 1974
85. Previously unpublished
86. *The New Yorker,*
    August 11, 1975
87. Previously unpublished
88. *Saturday Review,*
    November 15, 1975
89. *The New Yorker,*
    September 9, 1967
90. *The New Yorker,*
    November 22, 1969
91. *The New Yorker,* March 9, 1968
92. *The New Yorker,* March 1, 1976
93. *The New Yorker,* June 3, 1973
94. Previously unpublished
95. *The New Yorker,* March 1, 1969
96. Previously unpublished
97. Previously unpublished
98. Previously unpublished
99. Previously unpublished
100. Previously unpublished
101. Previously unpublished
102. *The New Yorker,* April 22, 1974
103. Previously unpublished
104. *The New Yorker,* March 21, 1971
105. *The New Yorker,* June 24, 1974
106. Previously unpublished
107. Previously unpublished
108. Previously unpublished
109. Previously unpublished
110. Previously unpublished
111. *The New Yorker,*
     February 3, 1973
112. *Sales Management,* 1969
113. *The New Yorker,*
     September 2, 1974
114. *The New Yorker,* June 28, 1976
115. *The New Yorker,* June 28, 1969
116. Previously unpublished
117. *Practical Psychology,*
     October 1975
118. *Better Homes & Gardens,*
     September 1975
119. *The New Yorker,* January 6, 1975
120. *Saturday Review,* June 19, 1971
121. *The New Yorker,* May 17, 1976
122. *Saturday Review,* April 19, 1975
123. *The New Yorker,*
     September 6, 1969
124. *The New Yorker,*
     November 8, 1969
125. Previously unpublished
126. *The New Yorker,*
     December 16, 1974
127. *The New Yorker,*
     October 22, 1973
128. *The New Yorker,*
     February 11, 1974
129. *The New Yorker,* April 19, 1976
130. *Saturday Review,* May 31, 1975
131. *The New Yorker,* May 20, 1974
132. Previously unpublished
133. *The Rotarian,* April 1975
134. *Practical Psychology,*
     January 1976
135. *Saturday Review,*
     September 12, 1972
136. *The New Yorker,* July 1, 1972
137. Previously unpublished
138. Previously unpublished
139. *The New Yorker,* August 30, 1969

140. Previously unpublished
141. Previously unpublished
142. *The New Yorker,* July 17, 1971
143. *The New Yorker,* August 4, 1975
144. *The New Yorker,* January 1, 1972
145. Previously unpublished
146. Previously unpublished
147. Previously unpublished
148. *The Rotarian,* February 1975
149. *The New Yorker,* April 30, 1966
150. Previously unpublished
151. *Saturday Review,*
     December 4, 1971
152. *The New Yorker,* October 8, 1966
153. Previously unpublished
154. *The New Yorker,*
     November 30, 1968
155. Previously unpublished
156. Previously unpublished
157. *The New Yorker,*
     December 20, 1969
158. Previously unpublished
159. *The New Yorker,*
     December 17, 1973
160. *Better Homes & Gardens,*
     December 1970
161. Previously unpublished
162. Previously unpublished
163. Previously unpublished
164. *Saturday Review,* January 3, 1970
165. Previously unpublished
166. *The New Yorker,*
     December 31, 1973
167. *Saturday Review,* May 4, 1974
168. *The New Yorker,*
     January 27, 1973
169. *The New Yorker,* July 8, 1974
170. Previously unpublished
171. Previously unpublished
172. *The New Yorker,* March 18, 1974
173. *Saturday Review,*
     October 24, 1970
174. *The New Yorker,* May 10, 1969
175. *The New Yorker,*
     January 30, 1971
176. *The New Yorker,* May 6, 1972
177. *The New Yorker,*
     December 26, 1970
178. *The New Yorker,*
     August 27, 1973
179. Previously unpublished
180. *The New Yorker,*
     September 23, 1967
181. *The New Yorker,*
     December 15, 1975
182. *The New Yorker,*
     September 24, 1973
183. *The New Yorker,*
     January 17, 1970
184. *The New Yorker,* April 25, 1970
185. *The New Yorker,*
     February 3, 1975
186. *The New Yorker,*
     December 12, 1970
187. *The New Yorker,* April 28, 1975
188. *The New Yorker,*
     December 2, 1967
189. *The New Yorker,*
     November 23, 1968
190. *The New Yorker,* August 2, 1969
191. *The New Yorker,* May 5, 1973
192. *The New Yorker,* March 6, 1971
193. *The New Yorker,*
     January 31, 1970
194. Previously unpublished